Kansas

By Christine Taylor-Butler

Subject Consultant
Dr. John Heinrichs, Associate Professor
Department of Geosciences
Fort Hays State University, Hays, Kansas

Reading Consultant
Cecilia Minden-Cupp, PhD
Former Director of the Language and Literacy Program
Harvard Graduate School of Education
Cambridge, Massachusetts

Children's Press®
A Division of Scholastic Inc.
New York   Toronto   London   Auckland   Sydney
Mexico City   New Delhi   Hong Kong
Danbury, Connecticut

Designer: Herman Adler Design
Photo Researcher: Caroline Anderson
The photo on the cover shows a Kansas farm.

Library of Congress Cataloging-in-Publication Data

Taylor-Butler, Christine.
  Kansas / by Christine Taylor-Butler.
      p. cm. — (Rookie Read-About Geography)
  Includes index.
  ISBN 0-516-24966-5 (lib. bdg.)   0-516-26454-0 (pbk.)
  1. Kansas—Juvenile literature. 2. Kansas—Geography—Juvenile literature.
I. Title. II. Series.
  F681.3.T39 2006
  917.81'02—dc22   2005021248

JE
TAY
c·1   7/06

CHILDREN'S PRESS, and ROOKIE READ-ABOUT®,
and associated logos are trademarks and/or registered trademarks
of Scholastic Library Publishing. SCHOLASTIC and associated logos
are trademarks and/or registered trademarks of Scholastic Inc.

1 2 3 4 5 6 7 8 9 10 R 15 14 13 12 11 10 09 08 07 06

Do you know why Kansas is called the Sunflower State?

Wild prairie sunflowers grow all over Kansas. The wild prairie sunflower is the state flower.

Kansas is located in the middle of the United States. Can you find Kansas on this map?

CANADA

WASHINGTON

MONTANA
NORTH DAKOTA
MINNESOTA
NEW HAMPSHIRE
VERMONT
MAINE

OREGON
IDAHO
SOUTH DAKOTA
WISCONSIN
MICHIGAN
NEW YORK
MASSACHUSETTS
RHODE ISLAND

WYOMING
NEBRASKA
IOWA
PENNSYLVANIA
CONNECTICUT
NEW JERSEY

NEVADA
UTAH
COLORADO
KANSAS
MISSOURI
ILLINOIS
INDIANA
OHIO
WEST VIRGINIA
DELAWARE
MARYLAND
Washington, D.C.

CALIFORNIA
ARIZONA
NEW MEXICO
OKLAHOMA
ARKANSAS
KENTUCKY
TENNESSEE
VIRGINIA
NORTH CAROLINA

SOUTH CAROLINA

TEXAS
MISSISSIPPI
ALABAMA
GEORGIA

LOUISIANA
FLORIDA

North
West   East
South

ALASKA   CANADA   MEXICO

HAWAII

5

The state bird is the
western meadowlark.

The state tree is the cottonwood. It grows along rivers and streams.

The northeast corner
of Kansas is called the
Dissected Till Plains.

Rivers and streams cut
through the land. This
creates high cliffs called
bluffs. The Dissected Till
Plains get a lot of rain.
The soil here is perfect
for farming.

The Kansas River joins the Missouri River in the east. The Kansas River is good for canoeing and fishing.

The Kansas and Missouri rivers join here.

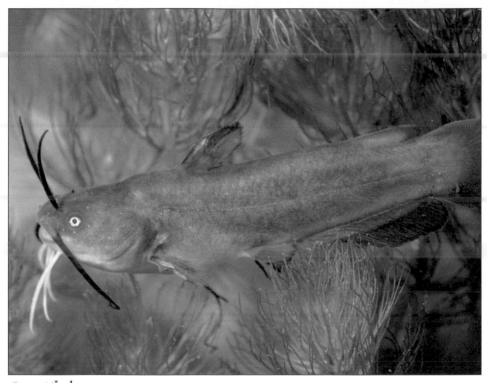

A catfish

Bass, catfish, and walleye live there.

The Osage Plains form the eastern half of Kansas. This area has rolling hills and lowlands.

Wheat is an important crop in the Osage Plains. Kansas grows more wheat than any other state.

The Flint Hills are to the west of the Osage Plains. Buffalo once roamed there.

Wheat farming on the Osage Plains

The Red Hills

Farther west are the Red Hills and the Smoky Hills. Soil and rocks in the Red Hills contain iron oxide. Iron oxide makes the land look red.

Wood is scarce in the Smoky Hills. Instead, a rock called limestone is found there.

Western Kansas is called the Great Plains. The land is flat and dry. Not much rain falls there. People dig wells to get water from the ground.

Prairie grass, cactus, and yucca plants grow in this area.

Yucca plants on the Great Plains

18

Mount Sunflower is the highest point in Kansas. It is a small hill near the Kansas–Colorado border. It rises more than 4,000 feet (1,200 meters).

The Arkansas River flows through Kansas. This river is almost 500 miles (800 kilometers) long. It is dry most of the year.

Sand dunes are found near the Arkansas River.

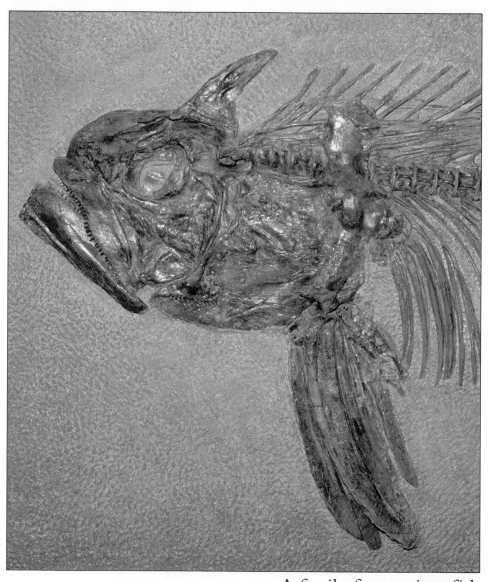

A fossil of an ancient fish

Millions of years ago, Kansas was covered by seas. Giant fish and dinosaurs once lived there.

Many fossils can be found in Kansas. Fossils are the hardened remains of plants or animals that lived long ago.

Topeka is Kansas's capital.
Kansas is the 13th-largest
state in the United States.

Wichita is the largest city in Kansas. It has many factories. Some of these factories make airplane parts.

NEBRASKA

COLORADO

Missouri River

Dissected Till Plains

Kansas City, Missouri

Great Plains

Smoky Hills

Kansas River

Kansas City, Kansas

Topeka ✪

△ Mount Sunflower

KANSAS

Osage Plains

Arkansas River

Wichita

Flint Hills

MISSOURI

Red Hills

SCALE 1 inch = 100 miles

0   Miles   100

0   Kilometers   160

OKLAHOMA

North
West   East
South

26

Kansas City, Kansas, is not far from Kansas City, Missouri. The two cities are separated by the Missouri River.

Sheep and hogs are raised near Kansas City, Kansas.

Maybe one day you will visit Kansas.

What will you do when you get there?

Words You Know

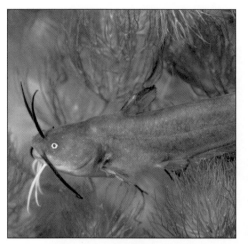

catfish

cottonwood

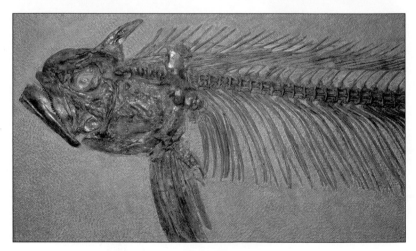

fossils

western meadowlark

wheat

wild prairie sunflowers

yucca plants

31

Index

About the Author

Christine Taylor-Butler is the author of twenty-one books for children. She is a graduate of the Massachusetts Institute of Technology. She is also the author of *Missouri* and *The Mississippi River* in the Rookie-Read-About® Geography series. Christine lives in Kansas City, Missouri, with her husband and two children.

Photo Credits

Photographs © 2006: Airphoto/Jim Wark: 10; Alamy Images/Tom Till: 17, 31 bottom right; AP/Wide World Photos: 29 (Richard Gwin/Lawrence Journal-World), 21 (Orlin Wagner); Carol Yoho/Dancing Goat Press, Topeka, KS: 18; Corbis Images: 13, 31 top right (Bettmann), 22, 30 bottom (Kevin Schafer); Dembinsky Photo Assoc./Gary Meszaros: 11, 30 top left; Getty Images/Larry W. Smith: 25; Photo Researchers, NY: 9 (John Buitenkant), 7, 30 top right (Kenneth M. Highfill), 14 (Larry Miller), 6, 31 top left (Rod Planck); Superstock, Inc.: cover (Americana Images), 26 (Richard Cummins), 3, 31 bottom left (MedioImages).

Maps by Bob Italiano